CW01589889

For Charlie and Milo

Contents

Introduction

Hi there, my name is Anna. By purchasing this book, you are already one step closer to being independent, taking charge of your time and setting up your own Dog walking service.

As a successful business owner, I decided to write this book to help other likeminded dog lovers create their own businesses doing what they love. When I first began my pet care service, it took a lot of research and determination to find all the relevant pieces of knowledge I needed to know in order to start my company. I found that information was not easily accessible and often contradicting. Now, dog walking as a business is not regulated by a professional body; as a result, this means that anyone can set up a pet care venture. However, to be a professional and set up your own organisation as a sustainable career, takes a little more that picking up a lead a taking a dog for a walk.

I hope that this book will act as a guide to support you in the creation of your business and make it much more accessible to find the important information and further reading suggestions. I aim to answer many asked questions and provide you with handy hints and tips gained through my experiences, should you need any further information or printable templates visit my website www.bigpoochlittlepooch.com.

I wish you every success in your new venture!

Anna

Chapter 1

Why dog walking– Am I cut out for it?

Why dog walking– Am I cut out for it?

Most people could be dog walkers; however, it takes determination, dedication and drive to make it as a successful small business owner. As a dog walker you see new dog walking businesses come and go. Usually as the hot weather arrives you see an increase in dog walkers who enjoy plodding through local parks and walk ways, it's as the really hot weather comes or similarly when the British norm of rain and wind presents itself that you see them quickly stop their walks and return to their previous lives.

Dog walkers are required to walk day and night come rain or shine. Clients rely on our regular services and so do their dogs. When starting your dog walking business, it is important to remember that you are your own boss. You can choose your working hours and you schedule your diary around to fit you. This was a novel idea when I first started dog walking and I never turned off. I would walk any dogs at any time often at sacrifice of my own plans. Time management and ownership of your time is covered further on in this book; though it is important to highlight this being a self-employed dog walker/small business owner does require hours of dedication, invoicing, advertising, correspondence to name but a few in addition to that of actually walking dogs, don't let this put you off though, the rewards you reap for the dedication is far greater.

It's not all doom and gloom, believe me there is nothing greater than collecting a dog for a walk who has been expecting you. The dog's happy wag and grateful expression can light up even the dreariest of days. Owners are all different as are all dogs. You are not obliged to take any dog/owner into your business if you do not feel the fit is right. You can, as with any job, be sometimes treated as a disposable commodity by owners, in this event remember the old mantra 'as one door closes-another opens'. Whilst it is sad to let a dog go who you have built a rapport up with; occasionally it is not worth the hassle of being talked down to or having to chase payments.

Most dog walkers are fortunate and never experience poor clientele, however they are out there and no matter the level of planning, contract signing and resourcing sometimes you have to think on your feet and stick up for yourself and what you have built. Fortunately, the majority of clients are appreciative of your service and ask advice and welcome support with the care of their furballs. It is important to remember in this case, to suggest guidance as we are not trained vets but can only share our own experiences; always refer owners to their own vet if they become worried or concerned about their pets.

A love for dogs and genuine compassion and care are essential to becoming a successful dog walker, a cheery disposition is always helpful too. Often owners use you as their personal agony aunt as you are an outsider in their everyday lives, and they find it easy to share their problems. Remember not to get too involved with the day to day lives of your clients; it doesn't hurt to lend a listening ear and show sympathy or care. Time and again the trust you build with your clients reinforces the trust they have in your when caring for their pets. It also doesn't hurt to go that extra mile when caring for their dogs, simple things like closing the curtains on dark evenings or popping a light on can make you stand out from the competition.

The more trustworthy and reliable you are, the better. It is advisable to obtain a Disclosure and Barring Service (DBS) certificate which you can show your clients upon meet and greet. This proves that you have a (hopefully) clean record and enforces your trustworthiness. Owners regularly trust their dog walkers with keys to their property so that you can collect their dogs in their absence for walks. If they are to give you a key, you need to reinforce that you are a trustworthy person who does not impose a threat to their home, belongings or pet. Sometimes, owners have key safes, this is becoming increasingly common now as owners employ cleaners and gardeners to maintain their properties due to their heavy work commitments. These are usually small boxes with a numeric combination which the owner should give you upon agreement of the contract, terms and conditions.

It is not essential but advisable to obtain a qualification in pet care. Make sure that it is a creditable qualification not a '.com' printable. This is more for your information in caring for pets than for impressing clients, though a little impressing is always good, once again it sets you ahead of the competition. Caring for dogs is not as simple as having just owned your own, there are many different types of dogs with different needs and ways of expressing their needs. I would suggest looking up animal behaviour courses as a place to start- see links in the reference section for more reading. Learning the basics in dog behaviour can help you predict conflicts, read situations and help to avoid and resolve issues that may arise.

Look into local accredited Dog First Aid courses. Once again this is not crucial but will guide you on what to do in an emergency when out and about with dogs on your own and will also put you ahead of the competition. Remember a large part of becoming a successful dog walker is being trusted to look after client's pets who are often treated like their children. Customers want the reassurance that you will treat their dogs like your own and that you are prepared for any eventuality to care for their loved one.

It would also be a good idea to get some animal care experience before embarking on your own business. Volunteers are always greatly appreciated. Try volunteering at your local vets or pet shelter. By doing this, you will gain a greater awareness to the different types of dogs and how people who are trained to deal with pets, do in fact handle situations. Not every scenario will be the same, as the variables will change but this would be a great opportunity to gain insight and start building your pet care toolkit of tricks.

Chapter 2

Advertising

Advertising

Advertising is an essential part of building your successful business. A huge part of advertising is Logo exposure. You need to design a logo that is eye catching and simple in design. Do not fall into the trap of logging onto websites that can design one for you and put it onto leaflets and other merchandise for you. The odds are that someone else local to you has already done this, resulting in you both having the same logo and thus showing a lack of originality. Whilst this option seems like a quick and easy solution, many of these facilities copyright the logos that they produce which prohibits you using the logo on your own merchandise, advertising and more importantly websites and social media.

Along with your Logo you also need a catchy name. I find google a useful tool here, you can google your ideas and see if they are already taken. You will find that most dog related names will already be taken, you want to be original to help you stand out. Try alliteration as it helps the name flow off the tongue and stick in people's heads. Consider using part of your name, this will increase the possibility of your name being more original. Use family and friends and brainstorm ideas. I made a game of it one evening whilst I had family over for food and drinks. Eventually, a business name was created, I like it and it stuck. This was the birth of my company Fenny's Furballs. Fenny as that is my surname, original as not many people have this surname and Furballs because it related to pets but added alliteration to my business name. I ran it though google and came up with no hits, this meant it was original, I would have access to email addresses, website domains and social media handles without the compromise of having to add additional numbers or letters to create accounts. It was catchy and different drawing attention and intrigue making people look further. Have a play, there is no right or wrong.

Advertising Leaflets need to be concise and eye-catching. Have a look at other dog walkers' adverts either online or in local magazines, see what other people have done. Which adverts are you drawn to and why? Consider the colours used in the advert, are they easy to read together? What fonts have been chosen? Have they used images? Keep in mind that you cannot just download images from google as they will be copyrighted. A great tool to help you get images is using Microsoft Publisher's images from the internet device. It enables you to find images that are for creative commons use 'CC'. These are images that licences that allow you to 'distribute, remix, adapt and build upon work, even commercially' on the proviso that you give credit to the original creator, Creative Commons Licences (2020). For more information on licensing and use of images and text visit the creative commons website.

Phone numbers and email addresses need to be for business use as this will be how your customers will contact you. I use my own phone number for work and for family however do use the do not disturb function to separate work and homelife, more on this in the working hours section. You email address needs to be easily accessible and preferably have the business name in it. A great free to use email domain is 'mail.com'. They make it easy to produce email addresses and play with the @... enabling you a huge degree of flexibility to create your email address. It is important to remember that you are creating a professional business and as a result need to present this professional image in all aspects of your business including that of voicemail recordings and email addresses.

There are many different methods of advertising, this becomes less necessary as you become established as your reputation tends to circulate by word of mouth or by existing clients liking and sharing your social media posts. There is much debate as to whether to start with professional printed leaflets or to just produce homemade printed leaflets. My advice would be to start home printed; you are only just starting your business and do not want to pay out for things until you start making money. If you have pre-saved for the launch of your business, professional printing may be an expense that you would consider but it is not essential.

The next step is based on being a little cheeky, if you do not ask-you don't know. Try asking local shops to post your leaflet in their shop window, the local post office is usually a good place too; sometimes they charge a minimal fee, but you need to consider the footfall that will pass your advert. A lot of elderly people use the post office which is a great target audience for you as they often need a little extra help walking their dogs. Pet shops, popular walking places and garden centres are great places to put up and advertising leaflet as they are places your target audience will frequent, especially those who work throughout the week and need pet care whilst they are at work.

Facebook marketplace and local Facebook selling groups are a brilliant free advertising resource. Lots of people peruse these sites at their leisure and can come across your advert by chance. If they are not looking for a dog walker, you can be sure that they know someone who has a dog; more about this in the websites and social media section of this book.

Many places now have local magazines which you can advertise your services in. These vary in prices and need to be considered carefully. Look at their target audiences and how they deliver. Think about their range of delivery too, what is their delivery radius? Does it cover the areas you wish to walk? Most magazines will give you a pay as you go option. Try it for a couple of months to see if your client interest increases. Just using a one-off edition isn't the best way to use this means as recipients of the magazine will flick through the adverts. It is when they hear that someone needs a dog walker or wants one themselves that they will remember they saw an advert and try and find it. As a result of this, it tends to pay to have a recurring ad for a couple of months. I personally have not had much success from adverts in magazines the costs of advertising outweighed the uptake of now clients. I have had more success from advertising via Google's pin my business on google maps.

Google Business is a fabulous way of gaining clients. It is free to use and for me has provided the greatest uptake. You register your business on google but do not choose their advertising – if you have the spare money too this would be an option as it can increase your exposure and put your website to the top of the list. By registering you pin your business on google maps, along with various search criteria that you come under. This now means that anyone who types into google 'dog walkers near me' or 'pet care [location]' your business will pop up. Try it yourself, see who your competition is and what they offer. How can you make your business more attractive than theirs?

Advertising Checklist

DBS

Qualification (optional)

Dog First Aid Certificate

Business Name

Business Logo

Business Phone Number/Voicemail

Business Email Address

Advertising Leaflet

Registered with Google Business

Doodle Page – Business Name Ideas

Doodle Page – Funky Logo Ideas

Chapter 3

Websites and Social Media

Websites and Social Media

Why do I need a website? This is a commonly asked question from many new dog walkers who are setting up their business. With today's modern age, the internet is one of the first places that people look. By having a website, it gives you a searchability when people are looking for a dog walker. It also provides you with a platform to sell your business, showcase what you do and what set you apart from the competition, list prices and services, contact information and give the owners a place to look for pictures of their beloved furballs.

There are several ways of creating a website, if you are particularly computer savvy, it would be worth building your own site using something like WordPress. I personally chose this method so that I did not have the fear of someone owning my work, pictures or property put on there; however it was not easy and still to this day takes me hours of hair pulling and coffee drinking to achieve my desired outcome. For those who would like to keep their head of hair intact there are alternatives out there.

There are many companies now that will build small businesses websites for a fee alternatively there are websites to create websites such as 'Wix.com', 'godaddy.com' and 'squarespace.com' to name but a few. These sites provide you with templates to complete and stock images that you can import into your website making the process much easier. You will have to check for copywriting on your website and their terms and conditions and how they might have an impact on you. Don't forget to name your website the same or something close to your business name and link it to your Google account for people to click on and follow the link.

If you are intending on putting up pictures of the dogs you walk on your website or any social media page, it would be advisable to get written permission and a signature allowing you to do so. I would suggest that you include this within your contract to make it easier but give this its own section with space for a signature. This way you are not publishing images without owner consent and can use them for advertising purposes and sections within your website. I decided to create a rogues gallery section on my website and regularly upload pictures of the furballs in my care, this not only shows the owners what their dogs are doing whilst out and about with you but advertises the activities you do with the dogs to new clients.

Social media is a very valuable tool these days. Using various social media platforms is a great way to publicise your business for free and get a wealth of exposure. This is where I found I gain most new clients (this and google search). Facebook is my main platform that I use. I have a business page which is created using your own Facebook login. Use the link 'https://www.facebook.com/business/pages/set-up' for more information on how to set up your Facebook business page. It needs to be set up in a similar way to your website to make for easy navigation but can be updated much quicker and easier than your website. I use my business Facebook in a 'blog' manner putting up need to know information for clients, today's pictures and helpful hints and tips.

Facebook is a great way to network with other dog walkers, there are many groups that you can join ask questions and share experiences with one another. This is invaluable for sharing of clients, if other dog walkers are fully booked but work in a similar area to you, they may post details of potential clients here too.

Like the group networking aspect of Facebook, the groups such as 'things for sale in my area' are a great place to put a post about your services. This is free to do but there are some Facebook rules which may inhibit certain wording or structure of your advert (double check these before posting).

Instagram is an instrumental social media platform which more and more people are using, particularly of the younger generation. It enables you to post up to 10 pictures in one post and link to other like posts using hashtags (see below). Instagram can be used as a stand-alone platform for business or can be linked to an existing personal account. Instagram enables your clients to 'follow' your business page and they will get notifications when you post something new. They can comment on posts that you put on and expresses virtual emotions to them.

Twitter is another helpful social media platform. Twitter enables you to link your personal twitter account with your business twitter account making this very simple to navigate between the two. You can also link your twitter and Instagram account to your Facebook account, reducing the amount of work you need to do to cover all social media bases.

Twitter and Instagram use the # (hashtag) system to link posts that are alike; by linking posts you are increasing your business exposure again for free. Hashtags links like the ones suggested below are a great place to start but try setting up your own hashtag trend *#Dogwalkingbusinessname.*

Suggested Hashtags for dog walkers

#Bigpoochlittlepooch

#walkies

#doginstagram

#puplife

#doggypals

#furballs

#pupdate

#dogwalker

#dogsofinsta

#moochthepooch

#adventurepups

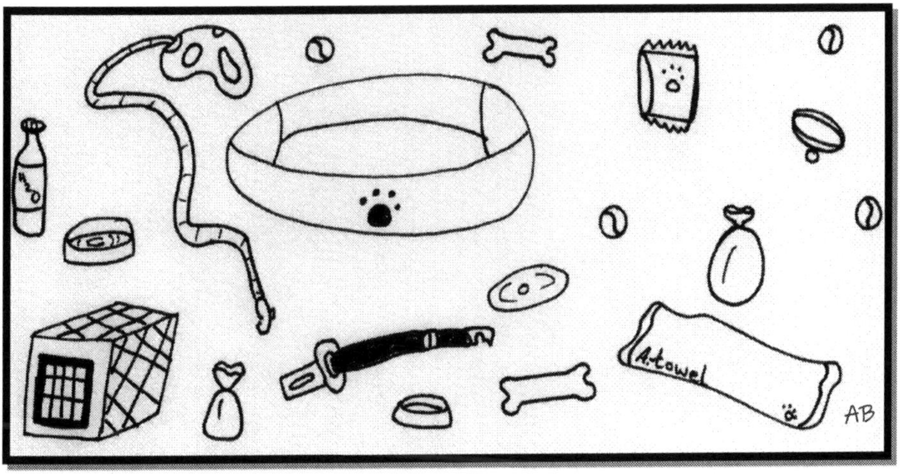

Chapter 4

What do I need?

What do I need?

It would be easy to assume one of two things when becoming a dog walker, either you don't need anything to set yourself up as a pet carer or the opposite that you need a coach load of equipment to care for the pets. In experience, it is somewhere in the middle. You need to be prepared for almost anything but in compact, easily accessible way. Your vehicle becomes your mobile office, as a result it is important to pack the essentials into your vehicle and keep them there for all walks. Most things will stay there in case of emergency, but I believe it is always best to be prepared for the worst-case scenario.

Old towels are a dog walking essential. Dogs always get wet and muddy, even on the hottest and driest of days. Old towels are great for absorption and easy to wash on a high heat to kill germs and bacteria. If you don't have any old towels to use, try asking on your local Facebook buying and selling page for free old towel donations. You will be surprised the amount of people that will respond.

It's always handy to have a couple of spare collars, just in case an owner forgets to leave one out for you or something happens to the dogs existing collar. It is a legal requirement for all dogs to wear an identification collar now as well as being microchipped. It is important to reiterate this to the owners on meet and greet (see meet and greet section for more details). Pop on a tag with your Business name and your contact number should the pet become lost; it will have some level of identification on it.

Water bowls, a bottle of water and dog friendly wet wipes are always handy to have in your vehicle. Not only to provide the dogs with a drink after their walk but to wash them down/wipe them if it was particularly muddy or a little darling has rolled in poo (Yes they do this, other dogs poo and wildlife poo is attractive to all dogs and they cannot resist having a good old roll if given the chance). Along with this it would be good to carry a selection of dog treats (check with the owners during meet and greet to see if the dog is allowed treats). Treats are not only good to reinforce positive behaviours but work well as bribery if you are in a pinch. Often if walked in a group, even the best-behaved dogs, get over excited at the prospect of being out and about with their furbuddies and can ignore instructions/commands. In this case, the promise of a treat being held out for them is enough to entice them back to you so that you can clip their lead on.

Balls and frisbees are great way to promote activity amongst the dogs. WARNING! Make sure you get to know the dogs if walking in a group before introducing balls other toys. Some dogs can be possessive and aggressive towards other dogs when toys are involved, so use your own initiative and introduce toys if appropriate. Like with the treats, dogs will respond to toys as a reward for good behaviour. I walk a dog who when he gets excited tends to want to be chased when playtime is over.
He does not want to return with the pack because he wants to play more.
I know that his weakness is for squeaky tennis balls, one squeak of the ball and he's galloping towards me at which point I do the quick latch of the lead and give him the ball. He is happy he has his ball and I am happy that he is back on his lead and I am in control.

It is important that you have a pet first aid kit in your vehicle along with a list of emergency contacts for the animals in your care see the proforma below for guidance on what you could include in your emergency list.

<table>
<tr><td>LOGO</td><td colspan="2">Name of Company</td></tr>
<tr><td colspan="3">Emergency Contact</td></tr>
<tr><td colspan="2">Name of Dog</td><td rowspan="2">[Picture of Dog]</td></tr>
<tr><td>Owner Name</td><td>Owner contact number</td></tr>
<tr><td>Emergency Contact Name</td><td>Emergency contact Number</td><td>Microchip Number</td></tr>
<tr><td colspan="2">Name of Vets</td><td>Known Health Issues/ Medication</td></tr>
<tr><td>Address of Vets</td><td>Vets contact Number</td><td>Insurance Number</td></tr>
</table>

Consider buying a first aid kit whilst on your first aid course (often they have them for sale), I also sell them on our website www.bigpoochlittlepooch.com or you could make your own using from the list below. This list is just recommendations taken from the PDSA website; www.pdsa.org.uk, seek further veterinarian advice if you are uncertain.

First Aid Kit Essentials

- Bandages
- Blunt-ended scissors
- Wound Wash
- Cotton Wool
- Tweezers
- Tick Tweezers
- Vet wrap
- Foil blanket
- Antiseptic wipes
- Wound Dressings
- Self-adhesive tape
- Thermometer
- Dressings
- Vinyl gloves

It goes without saying that as a dog walker it is your responsibility to provide poo bags and collect the faecal matter left by the dogs in your care. I like to use rolls of poo bags as it's a great way of having a lot of bags in your pocket at one time. Most pockets in my clothes have rolls of poo bags, make sure you check them before washing though – I have had many a poo bag perfectly cleaned by the washing machine (oops!). I feel that as a professional dog walker it is our job to promote positive dog walking etiquette. This includes collection of dog poo, correct disposal (if there is no bin, take it home) and positive dog walking habits for example, not just letting dogs run up to others that they don't know, leading them up and communicating with the other dog owner; see the Dog Walking Etiquette for more details.

Dog Walking Etiquette

DOG ON LEAD YOUR DOG OFF LEAD	BOTH DOGS ON LEAD	BOTH DOGS OFF LEAD

Do not let your dog approach the dog on lead. Call your dog away. This is called an 'uneven' meeting as it is unfair to the dog on the lead. *Remember* that there is usually a reason why a dog is on a lead, so give them space and leave them alone.	Ask permission from the other dog walker before approaching. Wait for them to answer. *Remember,* even if the dog walker says it is ok, approach with caution. Observe the body language of the dogs. If they say no, give them space and move on quickly and quietly.	If you are close enough, ask permission from the other dog walker. *Remember,* be careful with toys and treats around other dogs. This could create friction and lead to possessive behaviour. Supervise heavily and watch the dogs body language.

What do I need Checklist

- ◊ Old Towels
- ◊ Spare Leads both flexi and flat for different sized dogs
- ◊ Spare collar with dog tags
- ◊ Water Bowl
- ◊ Water Bottle
- ◊ Treats
- ◊ Balls/Frisbee
- ◊ Poo bags (biodegradable)
- ◊ Pet friendly wet wipes
- ◊ Dog first aid kit
- ◊ Emergency contact lists and veterinarian release forms

(see contract section for more info)

Chapter 5

Transport & Transport Safety

Transport & Transport Safety

It is essential that you have some type of transport, but you do not need a van straight away. It is many people's assumption that you need one to be a dog walker, this is not true. It is helpful to have a van for a number of reasons such as to save your car from getting damaged, to increase the quantity of dogs you can transport at one time and to make it easier to clean out. Like most dog walkers started in my own car and eventually 'graduated' to using a business van.

You need a car in order to get from one house to another, if you are doing group walks, then it is essential to transport the animals around between their homes and the place you are going to walk them. There are many things you can purchase to try and keep your car intact whilst transporting often wet and muddy dogs for example boot liners, rubber mats, seat protectors and old towels. These items are inexpensive but help save the fabric of the seats and make it easier to clean and maintain.

It is important to mention that there are strict laws in relation to the transportation of animals. Dogs must be either tethered by a doggy seat belt harness, put into crates or situated in the boot behind a dog guard. Different councils have different specifications but the basics remain the same (rule 57 of the highway code), the animal must be
'suitably restrained so they cannot distract you while you are driving or injure you or themselves if you stop quickly.' Department for Transport (2019).

Obviously, it goes without saying that your vehicle should have an up to date MOT, be regularly maintained/serviced and have full business use insurance which includes the transportation of animals.

It would also be advisable to provide window blinds during hot months to keep the sun off the animals and remember not to leave dogs unattended in the car on a warm day, even with the windows down as this could lead to not only poor health for the dogs but a prosecution for you under the animal welfare act (2006).

Transport and Safety Checklist

- ◊ Dog Boot Liner
- ◊ Doggy seat belts
- ◊ Seat protector
- ◊ Blankets/Old towels
- ◊ Dog Guard
- ◊ Crates/cage (size appropriate)

Chapter 6

Clothing- what to wear?

Clothing- what to wear?

When thinking about your clothing choices for dog walking you need to think practically. You are going to get muddy and dirty daily and will need flexibility. My advice is to think about layers as the Great British weather is very unpredictable. I have known it to be warm and sunny one minute and the next a torrential thunderstorm.

Fitness clothing tends to be the most convenient for this type of job as the trousers are generally made for flexibility and movement, the tops for breathability and comfort. Fleece jackets are usually good for dog walking as they keep you warm but are not bulky, many waterproof coats come with a fleece insert making it easier to fit a fleece inside a waterproof coat. As your business progresses or if budget allows it's a great idea to get your business logo either printed or embroidered onto them for additional advertising and professional appearance. This is not essential however just a bonus.

It is paramount that you invest in some good quality walking boots as you will be coving a fair distance daily. The support of a good walking boot will make the difference between you walking in comfort on all terrain and getting blisters and soggy feet. If it is forecast heavy rain or snow, then you may want to think about investing in a decent pair of wellington boots. My mistake was to buy a pair of fashionable ankle wellies, these do not stand up to lots of rain and muddy dogs splashing around as the water can get in easier! If, like me, you have 'shapely' calves and struggle to get longer wellies to fit, try muck boots as they have stretchy neoprene tops which hug your calves no matter what shape or size

Another sensible investment is waterproof trousers. These are readily available at most outdoor clothing shops. Remember you are going to be out in all weathers for a considerable amount of time. Not only do they keep your legs dry, but they also protect against wind chill. They are great for the cooler months and fold up small to keep in your vehicle.

I would advise a set of clothing for each day of the week. You will get wet and dirty, even if its glorious weather outside, dogs can find mud and water in the driest of places. Consequently, it would be helpful to have a change of clothes to reduce your daily washing. Similarly, it would be helpful to have a couple of waterproof coats, if you got soaked the day before it can take a while for the coat to dry out therefore having an alternative would be handy. Same with footwear as drying takes time.

It is tempting during hot weather to wear shorts, summer dresses and sandals when out walking but this would not be advisable. Sandals do not protect your feet and would not be suitable to a high amount of walking. Shorts do not protect your legs from dogs' claws (if jumping up) and plants whilst out on walks such as nettles. Like shorts, summer dresses do not protect you like full leg coverage and can, if floaty, trap insects in towards your legs such as mosquitoes, horse flies, bees and wasps.

You want to protect yourself in the best way possible as you are an essential part of your business, without you, there would be no business. Make sure to wear sun cream and hats during hot weather and warm scarves, gloves and woollen hats in the winter.

Clothing Checklist

Comfortable, stretchy trousers
Sturdy (waterproof) footwear
T-shirt (logo?)
Fleece/jumper
Waterproof Coat
Waterproof Trousers
Weather appropriate protection

Chapter 7

Weather and its Extremes

Weather and its extremes

Weather in the UK as we all know is extreme. It varies greatly throughout the year and brings with it its own challenges depending on the conditions.

Warm weather is particularly harmful to dogs, it is important that warm weather precautions are put in place and that both you and your clients are clear on the expectations and limitations of pet care during this time .

The usual mantra for walking dogs in the heat is to test the pavement with the back of your hand. If you cannot bare it for more than 20 seconds it is far too hot to allow your dogs to walk on it. Grass stays cooler than paths so if you must walk the dogs, do so on grass and if possible, in the shade of trees. Every dog is different in hot weather both large and small dogs come with their own issues, it is worth researching how heat effects different breeds as it is often surprising what effects different dogs. Dogs do not die from not having a walk, it is important to remember that you do not have to walk them in extreme weather but allow them the opportunity to go to the toilet and have access to essentials such as water.

It's not just the hot weather that can cause harm to dogs. Cold weather can be just as dangerous. As with the hot weather, make sure that you inform your clients as to your walking expectations during cold weather. It is not unreasonable to curtail walks if it is too hot or cold and I would insist on the dog having a coat of some description if it is icy and snowing.

Use caution during predicted storms too. I will never walk a dog in a thunderstorm. Not only are the dogs scared by the flashes and noise, I am too! The dogs are more likely to bolt or become aggressive to escape due to fear. If you are also worried, the dogs can sense this behaviour and can increase their reactions. In this scenario, allow them access to the toilet and sit with them. Put the radio on as a distraction, shut the curtains/ blinds and make a den if possible, using the towels left out by the client. I would also text the client to explain what you have done and why. Often, they are understanding and appreciative that you have taken the time to settle their pet. Our website www.bigpoochlittlepooch.com offers detailed documentation that includes the extreme weather conditions into dog walking contracts, terms and conditions.

Chapter 8

Rules and Regulations

Rules and Regulations

When it comes to dog walking, there are not many fixed rules and regulations to abide by. Most are advisory recommendations however there are some guidelines which we should look to follow. These guidelines have been taken from various sources such as the RSPCA, Dogs Trust, PIF (Pet industry Federation), CFSG (Canine and Feline sector group and DEFRA (Department for Environment, food and rural affairs).

There is an expectation that all dog walkers are suitably equipped for the job and have a competent knowledge of caring for dogs and dog behaviours. It is suggested by the Professional Dog Walker's guidelines that a dog walker should be qualified to at least City and Guilds level 2 in either canine behaviours of dog walking business. This, as previously mentioned is what sets professional dog walkers apart from the amateur.

As a dog walker, you are responsible for checking all equipment and its suitability for the animal it is intended for before each walk. In addition to this, you should not act in any way which would cause 'fear, anxiety or distress'. It is advisable that you should vary the dogs walk to increase interest and mental stimulation whilst out on walks whilst giving the dog your full attention to maintain control. Should you wish to let a dog off lead, you must obtain written permission from the owner prior to letting the dog off the lead. Off lead walking, once permitted, is to your discretion. It must be safe to do so and not by a public highway. You must also demonstrate control and ensure that the dog has full recall. You should keep the public safe and not let the dog rush up to other humans or dogs to ensure safety for all. Should you be unable to walk a dog off lead, it is advised that the dog be walked calmly on a loose lead, maintaining an appropriate length for the situation in which it is being walked.

There are exceptions to this rule where you must walk dogs on lead. An example of this would be if you are asked to lead walk a dog by an officer or dog warden. Below is an example sign which is displayed in my local parks and walking spaces, but most districts have a variant of their own. This sign has been taken from North West Leicestershire.

Another exception are Bitches that are in season, if needing to be walked, must be done so in a quiet area alone and on lead. Written permission for the walking of bitches on heat must be obtained from the owner. I personally do not walk bitches on heat as it is dangerous for both me and her. Male dogs when they sense a bitch on heat will try to get to her at all costs, dogs have been known to break through doors and fences to gain access to bitches, this I feel could lead to a level of aggression towards the bitch and could result in a dangerous situation. I would advise you to do your research carefully, check your business insurance terms and conditions and walk them at your own risk.

If walking dogs in a group, it is your responsibility to ensure that all animals are vaccinated and up to date with their flea and worm treatment. I do this by requesting and copy of the dog's vaccination records or copy of the titre test annually to have a record of the dogs' vaccinations. You should also ensure that all dogs who are walked together are suitably matched be it size, personality and gender. Experience helps here as you get a feel for the dogs who you are walking and can judge who would pair up well and who would not. I always find having an extra set of hands is valuable when introducing new dogs together. It enables you to carefully watch the body language and pull them apart should the meeting not go well.

The number of dogs you can walk at one time is regularly debated among dog walking professionals. The code of conduct recommends no more than 4 at one time. The actual amount can be dictated by your local authority and or your insurance provider. It is worth checking with both to ensure that you are not infringing any legislation.

As dog walkers, we have a responsibility to report any health, behaviour or welfare issues back to the owner and carefully and to make every effort to leave the dogs in a comfortable state upon return. Ensuring that they have access to water and are towelled down after walks is important. You should also make sure that the property is securely locked, and you have followed the client's instructions on exiting the property.

In the Further Reading section is a list of regulations and legislation that would be interesting to read. It would be advised to familiarise yourself with the contents and use them as a further guide when writing your contracts, terms and conditions and planning your services.

It is paramount that your business follows the rules and regulations of the data protection act and GDPR. All documents must be held in accordance to the 8 principles of which are highlighted on the following table.

For more information on rules and regulations and how you can apply these to your dog walking business, visit our website at www.bigpoochlittlepooch.com.

The GDPR Principles	
Processing Personal Data Fairly and Lawfully	**Processing Personal Data for Specified Purposes**
1 Principle 1 states that, the data must be legally processed, it must be lawful and fair to use, and that consent of the data subject must be transparent.	2 According to this principle, the data that is collected should not be used for unspecified reasons. For usage outside the specified purpose, a revision in consent it required.
Limit the Amount of Personal Data you hold	**Keeping Personal data Accurate and Current**
3 The data that you collect must be minimised in relation to the amount you gather. Only essential data should be collected.	4 The data you hold must be current and up to date. It should not be altered or manipulated to promote a misleading message.

The GDPR Principles Cont.

Retaining personal data with a set time frame.

5 The data you collect, and hold should be time limited. This means that the data should at some point be deleted or disposed of after a time has elapsed. [Most local authorities advise holding data for a maximum of 3 years].

Safeguarding the rights of individuals

6 The rights of the individuals to access their data should be entertained immediately and effectively.

Providing information security

7 The security of the information must be maintained. It should not pose a risk to the data subject.

The Exception

8 There is another clause in the GDOR that is occasionally considered the eight principle. It limits the transfer of data outside the EEA.

For more information on the Data Protection Act and GDPR visit www.gov.uk/dataprotection.

Chapter 9

Contracts & Terms and Conditions

Contracts & Terms and Conditions

A dog walking contract will provide transparency and create boundaries and clear expectations between you and your clients. It's important for a potential client to understand the services you provide, the price, and the terms and conditions of using your service. Your contract will also help you to manage all clients using the same rules and guidelines. Ensure to review dog walking contract with each client to help determine if your service is the right fit for them. It is important to highlight key aspects within your contract are you are working through it with them and to answer questions as you go along.

It is imperative that within your contract you highlight the policies and procedures of your business and what happens should that have to create last minute appointments, have to cancel, if there is adverse weather conditions and medical emergencies to name but a few. Make sure that your contract is clearly set out and addresses each point carefully.

Another essential part of your contract is to highlight the costs for your services and the different options that they can choose from. If you offer more than one service for example 1-hour dog walks and 30 min dog walks, make sure to explain the difference between the two as you discuss the contract and emphasise the price differences.

In addition to this, it is crucial that you obtain a veterinary release form from the clients. This is to ensure that you have written permission for the treatment of their pet should there be an emergency incident. It should highlight their permission, an emergency contact and who is responsible for paying the treatment. Some business insurers do cover emergency pet care, however it would be advisable to make the owner cover the costs and inform their veterinarian that you are the regular dog walker for their pet and have permission to discuss the pet's care with them. An example veterinary release form can be found on the next page. Downloadable editable contracts, terms and conditions and veterinary release forms are available from our website at www.bigpoochlittlepooch.com.

You should also outline in your contract a few other house rules and regulations. For example, do you have permission to walk the dog off-lead? If anything were to happen when the dog was off-lead and it transpired the owner had not agreed to it, your dog walking business could be held liable. This should be a signed permission. Similarly, you need to obtain publishing permission for photos and videos taken of their animals.

<table>
<tr><th colspan="3">Sample Veterinary Release Form</th></tr>
<tr><td>Owners Full Name</td><td colspan="2">Contact Telephone Number</td></tr>
<tr><td colspan="3">Owners Address</td></tr>
<tr><td>Emergency Contact Name</td><td colspan="2">Emergency Contact Number</td></tr>
<tr><td>Pet Name</td><td colspan="2">Pet DOB</td></tr>
<tr><td>Pet Description</td><td colspan="2">Medical Conditions</td></tr>
<tr><td>Pet Microchip Number</td><td colspan="2">Insurance Company and Policy Number</td></tr>
<tr><td colspan="3">TO WHOM IT MAY CONCERN
I hereby authorise the attending veterinarian to treat any of my pet as listed above and I accept full responsibility for all fees and charges incurred in the treatment of any of my pet.

[Company name] has permission to transport my pet(s) to and from the veterinary clinic for treatment or to request “on-site” treatment if deemed necessary. If I cannot be reached in case of an emergency, the walker shall act on my behalf to authorize any treatment excluding euthanasia.

I give permission to approve treatment up to [client to enter amount here].

I will assume full responsibility upon my return for payment and/or reimbursement for veterinary services rendered up to the above stated amount.</td></tr>
<tr><td>Dog Owner Name</td><td>Dog Owner Signature</td><td>Date</td></tr>
</table>

Sample Dog Walking Contract

Insert Logo Here

CLIENT DETAILS:

Client's Name ....

Client's Address ....

Post Code ....

Telephone Number ....

Emergency Contact Details:

Name ....

Numbers ....

Email address ....

I give permission for my dog's name and photograph to be used on social media and the **[Company Name]** website ☐	I **do/ do not** give my full consent for my dog(s) to be walked off lead. Signed ______________________

DOG DETAILS:	DOG DETAILS:
Dog's Name	Dog's Name ....
Breed and Age .... /	Breed and Age .... / ....
Sex male ☐ female ☐ Neutered/Spayed ☐	Sex male ☐ female ☐ Neutered/Spayed ☐
Fully Vaccinated Yes ☐ No ☐	Fully Vaccinated Yes ☐ No ☐
Collar with ID tag Yes ☐ No ☐	Collar with ID tag Yes ☐ No ☐
Microchipped Yes ☐ No ☐	Microchipped Yes ☐ No ☐
Health Notes	Health Notes ....
Behaviour Notes	Behaviour Notes ....
Insured Yes No Insured By .... Policy Number..	Insured Yes No Insured By .... Policy Number..

Insert Logo Here

Sample Dog Walking Consent Form

Dog Walking Contract Terms and Conditions

1.Relationship and Responsibilities

1.1 All dogs will be exercised on a lead unless prior agreement has been reached with **[Company Name]** and a disclaimer form has been signed.

1.2 **[Company Name]** will apply personal judgement and cut short a walk if necessary, because of extreme weather conditions (i.e., heat, thunder storms) for the safety of both the dogs and **[Company Name]**.

1.3 Your dog must wear a collar and ID tag and suitable harnesses, collars and leads as approved by **[Company Name]** as well as coats or muzzles if required. **[Company Name]** will provide fresh water, treats (if allowed) and toys during every session.

1.4 If dogs require a quick towelling off after walks towels must be provided and left by the front door.

1.5 All dogs must be up to date with their vaccinations. Kennel Cough vaccine is also highly recommended.

1.6 **[Company Name]** reserves the right to walk other compatible dogs at the same time but undertakes to limit the number of dogs walked with one person to 4 (Four). To be in a group walk, dogs must be over the age of 6 months and must be neutered or spayed. (Group walking is not available for non-neutered males over 6 months old or non-spayed females in season. Solo walking is recommended for them).

1.7 **[Company Name]** will supply and be equipped with a scooper/waste bags and will duly remove the dog's faeces from all public places.

2. Payment, Cancellation and Early Termination

2.1 I agree to pay **[Company Name]** in full either in advance or upon collection of the dog prior to the walk.

2.2 Either party may terminate this Dog Walking Contract a minimum of 24 (twenty-four) hours prior to the first scheduled visit without incurring penalties or damages.

2.3 Cancellation by the Owner of scheduled walks with less than 24 hrs notice may be charged at the full rate or rescheduled at the discretion of **[Company Name]**.

2.4 Where **[Company Name]** as sole proprietor needs to cancel a scheduled walk due to unforeseen circumstances; he/she may appoint a substitute Walker with the written approval of the Owner and any difference in the fees charged shall be for the account of **[Company Name]**.

2.5 Should any dog become aggressive or dangerous, **[Company Name]** may terminate this dog walking contract with immediate effect.

2.6. Any wrongful or misleading information in the Owner's Information or Pet Information sheets may constitute a breach of terms of this Dog Walking Contract and be grounds for instant termination thereof.

2.7. Termination under the circumstances described in 2.5 or 2.6 above shall not entitle the Owner to any refunds nor relief of any outstanding payments due.

3. Liability

3.1 **[Company Name]** accepts no liability for any breach of security or loss of or damage to the Owner's property if any other person has access to the property during the term of this agreement.

3.2 **[Company Name]** shall not be liable for any mishap of whatsoever nature which may befall a dog or caused by a dog who has unsupervised access to the outdoors.

3.3 The Owner shall be liable for all medical expenses and damages resulting from an injury to **[Company Name]** caused by the dog as well as damage to the Owner's property.

3.4 **[Company Name]** is released from all liability related to transporting dog(s) to and from any veterinary clinic or kennel, the medical treatment of the dog(s) and the expense thereof.

Sample Dog Walking Consent Form Continued.

Insert Logo Here

4. Emergencies

In the event of an emergency;

4.1 I authorise **[Company Name]** to obtain any emergency veterinary care that may be necessary during the time spent with my dog(s). I understand that every effort will be made to contact me prior to obtaining emergency care. I accept responsibility for any charges related to this emergency care. I also authorise **[Company Name]** to use an alternative veterinarian if my regular veterinarian is unavailable.

4.2 I will be responsible for any medical expenses and damages resulting from an injury to the dog walker or other persons/animals by my dog(s). I agree to indemnify and hold harmless **[Company Name]** in the event of a claim by any person injured by my dog(s).

5. Security

5.1 I agree to provide/arrange for keys to be available for **[Company Name]** ahead of the dog walking appointment. **[Company Name]** warrants to keep safe and confidential all keys, remote control entry devices, access codes and personal information of the Owner and to return same to the Owner at the end of the contract period or immediately upon demand.

6. Publications

6.1. Photos may be taken to be used on **[Company Name]** website and Facebook page.

7. Declaration

Print name: ....

Signed: .... **Dated:** ....

[Company Name] Signed: ....

Chapter 10

Home Visits/Meet and greets

Home Visits/Meet and greets

When going on home visits/meet and greets it is extremely important someone knows where you are going and roughly how long you expect to be. In addition to this, ensure that you dress professionally but appropriately. I am not saying wear a suit but look smart and presentable. If you have braded clothing with your logo on, wear it. Give the impression that you are a professional not just someone who has walked off the street. Confidence is important when meeting new people. Do not be conceited but confident in who you are, what service you are providing and that you are a professional in your field. If you do not feel confident, use the old mantra of 'fake it until you make it'; this has been proven to work, if you act like you are confident, the confidence will come naturally.

Prior to your visit do a little homework. Look at the location that the potential client lives in and how their location relates to where you live and the walks that you already do. Ask the clients about popular walking places that they frequent (you might find somewhere new) and discuss where you intend to take their dog on their walks. When discussing dog walks with your prospective clients look at your diary space and where they will fit into it. Give the owners a dog walking window, this gives you flexibility when walking other dogs so that they do not expect you at an exact time but during a time frame (a bit like a shopping delivery window).

When going to your meet and greet it is important that you take certain things with you. It would be a good idea to take a business card with you with your contact details on. Many potential clients will have found your details online so having a physical card with your information on is always handy; it also means that if someone mentions to them that they are looking for a dog walker, they have your details to pass on. In addition to this, you should take copies of your DBS certificate, Business insurance and qualifications.

It's always good to prove you are who you say you are, remember you are trying to gain trust with your potential clients. As well as this, take a spare copy of your contract and veterinary release form. You may want to email these to the client ahead of time for them to print and complete, but it is worth taking a spare in case something is missing.

Read though the contracts together and answer any questions they may have as you go along, feel free to make notes on the contract as a reminder of what has been said. Ensure you highlight key points in the contract and the expectations you have for the owners such as leaving out a dog towel, giving you access to a hose pipe, dog coats available etc. Make sure to have your mobile phone charged for the meeting, you can then take a copy of the dog's vaccination record and a picture of the dog for your records.

Make sure to discuss payment and expectations. When and how do you expect to be paid? Do you have a payment deadline which the client needs to be aware of? How will you send your invoices? Take a key ring with you. If the owners are happy with you and you with them, they will need to give you a house key (unless they have a key safe). This shows that you are prepared and that you take their security seriously.

Discuss social media and how the dog's pictures will be used, remember to get written consent for this. Furthermore, talk about the booking procedure, how do they book with you? Do you want a fixed day every week? Are you flexible with days?

It is important to mention that you do not have to take any dog onto your books, even if you have completed a meet and greet. You are interviewing the family and their dog, just as much as they are interviewing you. If you do not feel that their dog will fit with your walks, or feel that they do not fit your ethos, simply tell them that you do not feel that you are the best walker for them. If you are uncertain, maybe take the dog for a trial walk or meet the clients on a neutral ground for a walk. Ultimately, if you do not feel that the fit is right, simply walk away. There is always a need for dog walkers and as one door closes another will open. If you are networking with other dog walkers in the area, you may be able to give the client a few other dog walkers names and refer them on. This leaves the situation in good favour and gives them an opportunity to find another dog walker.

Home Visit Checklist

- ◊ Copy of Insurance certificate
- ◊ Contract
- ◊ Veterinary Release Form
- ◊ Terms and Conditions
- ◊ First Aid Certificate
- ◊ DBS Certificate
- ◊ Business Card

Chapter 11

Me, myself and I

Me, myself and I

Whilst being a dog walker is a fantastic profession giving your responsibility for your own hours and ways of doing things, it is also very important to consider you and your needs. It is very easy to be altogether consumed by your business and leave very little time for anything else.

When I started my business I worked 7 days a week between the hours of 9am and 8pm (not counting the hours after 8pm where I would dedicate time to invoice writing, contract writing, setting up of meetings, promoting on social media and emailing). After a while it became apparent that I was missing out on family time and never had time for myself. In the end, I made the hard decision to only work 5 days a week (Monday to Friday as these were the most requested days), giving me the weekend free. Eventually, I learnt that I also had to utilise the do not disturb function on my phone to force me to turn off at certain times and let after hours calls go to voice mail.

When you have your own business, you put all your time and effort into the creation of your little business baby. It is easy to forget the existence of a work-life balance, which is most people's reasons for becoming self-employed in the first place. Learn from my mistakes and give yourself working hours and stick to them, you need to have a life and time to do things for you to support your positive mental wellbeing.

As a dog walker, you are often a lone ranger, working by yourself. It is important to protect yourself not only by being insured and by having public liability but by implementing simple protection steps to ensure your safety whilst traversing the countryside alone.

It is paramount that your mobile phone is fully charged when you embark upon your dog walks and is advisable that you keep a charger in your vehicle. It would also be wise to download a personal tracking app which can alert others to your whereabouts should you get into difficulty. The tracking apps are also helpful, if you are like me and trek off and get lost in the middle of a field or woodland. They can plot your route which you can follow back to your starting point. Pre-programming emergency contacts on your phone would also be sensible should you find yourself in trouble. Many mobile phones have an emergency function where you can program in emergency contacts, next of kin, medications etc. These are great should you be found unconscious or unable to communicate as the paramedics are trained to look for these emergency bits in your phone. Another simple protection would be to have your next of kin registered in your phone as ICE (in case of Emergency) next to their name.

It would be prudent to have a daily diary of who you are collecting for walks and where they are; inform your emergency contact of the locality of the list. Should you get into trouble, rescuers would know a rough location for you. Similarly, having a first aid kit along with a rape alarm would be handy to have in a small dog walking bag, you could also keep your doggy poo bags and phone in there too.

Furthermore, it is important to have fully vehicle recovery cover. This goes without saying that they can help if there is a problem with your vehicle and help you get home. There is however many a grey area in the support offered for people with animals in the vehicle. It is worth checking with your breakdown provider to see what their protocol is relating to the recovery of livestock within a broken-down vehicle. In addition to this it is important to note that regular breakdown cover does not apply to business vans and needs to be taken out in its own separate policy.

Finally, it is important to remember that you are not alone. Utilise the social media pages for dog walkers and network. If you have a query about where to walk or want guidance on a problem, many are keen to help and advice from their experiences. If they don't know they often suggest where to look for answers to who to ask.

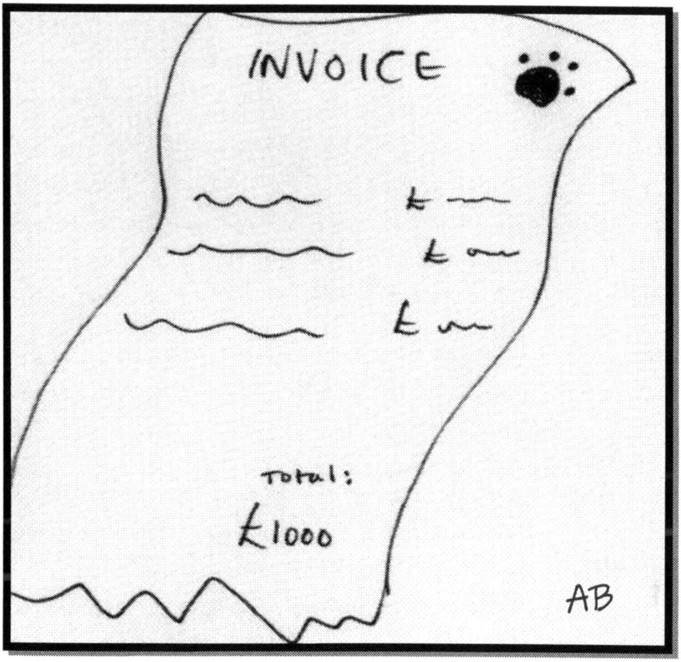

Chapter 12

Invoicing & Payment

Invoicing & Payment

Invoicing for payment is a crucial part of your business. It creates a paper trail of the work you have completed, and the payments owed by each client. It enables you to track your payments and ensure that your client clearly understands the costs of your services and where/how to pay. It is important that you clearly write when payment is expected by to comply with your business contract/terms and conditions and that failure to do so would be in breach of these terms. Downloadable, editable invoices are available at our website www.bigpoochlittlepooch.com. By creating invoices, it also enables your accountant or you to be able to easily complete your end of year tax return.

When it comes to payment it is up to you how much you charge. I would look at the surrounding businesses and find out how much they charge. You want to be competitive but not too cheap. A general guide (March 2020) is that an hour walk in the east midlands costs between £10.50 and £12.50, but this will be area and time dependant.

There are 3 main methods of payment, it is up to you to decided which one suits you better. All have pros and cons which I have detailed below. In addition to this, you must decide when the client is to pay you. Do you want payment before your service? Do you want monthly payments on a set date? Do you want weekly payments? All payment deadlines again come with positives and negatives but ultimately it is up to you to decide which works better for you.

Payment in advance ensures that you have the money before you provide the service, however many clients do not feel comfortable with this. Monthly payments mean that you must wait a whole month for your payments and risk running up a sizeable invoice for the client who may not pay at the end of the month (not everyone is an honest payer). Weekly invoicing works best for me as I do not run up such a large amount owed to chase for payment.

Sometimes, you need to chase payments and remind people that payments are still owed. Most pay promptly but you do have an occasional poor payer. I usually work on a '3 strikes and out' policy. If they are poor payers and do not correspond with you about payment, you are within your right to terminate your contract with them either until payment is received or indefinitely. Remember, you are the boss of your company and what you say goes. See more on this in the 'tough cookie' section of this book.

Pros and Cons regarding types of payment in my opinion.

Type of Payment	**Pros +**	**Cons -**
Cash	+ Cash in hand payment +Physical handling of money	-Must put the payment through the bank. -Need a secure place to store cash at home.
Bank Transfer	+ Direct into the bank account +No direct handling of money +Evidential tracking of money transactions	-No physical payment received -Must be regularly tracked to ensure payment has been made
PayPal	+Payment protection for both parties +Evidential tracking of money transactions +No direct handling of money	-Delay in transfer to your own bank account -Must be regularly tracked to ensure payment has been made -Can incur costs

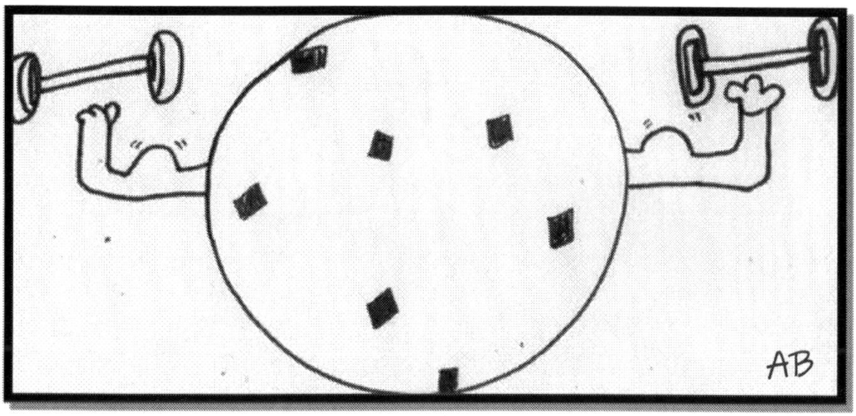

Chapter 13

Tough Cookie

Tough Cookie

Being an independent business owner is hard. You must make important decisions and stick to them. When I first started my dog walking business, I felt embarrassed about asking for money for my services. I felt that I was not worth the amount I was quoting for and was easily pushed around by some potential clients asking for deals and reduced rates. I was inexperienced and despite feeling prepared wasn't mentally prepared to stick up for myself and my business that I was building. I have since learnt that YOU and only you are in control of your business. You set the prices (to compete with others) and are worth every penny of what you ask for. If potential clients ask for discounts or deals, the odds are that they are not worth taking on. If they are questioning your prices now, are they going to continue to pay reliably. Remember, you don't go to the local supermarket and ask for a deal on their toilet paper, you just pay it and accept the price.

Self-worth is important in this line of work. You are building your business up from nothing and putting your heart and soul into this. Judgement and criticism can hurt but remember only your opinion counts. I have in the past had verbally abusive clients, clients who do not pay promptly as they see 'dog walkers' as a disposable commodity. People forget that if you are a professional dog walker, this is your job, your livelihood and just like with the supermarket analogy, you are providing a service which must be paid for. If you do get clients like this, make sure that you pursue your payment. If the outstanding figure is significant, you can always take them to small claims court; with the completion of your comprehensive contract and invoicing you will have the full support you need. Some dog walking business insurers also offer support should you need it. It is important to remember that there are always more clients, despite building up a bond with their dog, your time is money and you deserve to be paid and supported by your clients.

Some dog walkers are very territorial over their area of business and the dogs that they walk. They are not willing to network and share ideas and help one another. Do not be disheartened by this, healthy business that want to grow and develop do share questions and answers, they network and support one another. Facebook is a great networking tool with other professionals across the world. There are many groups and forums which you can join, ask questions and help others. Its also a great place to go if your confidence has been knocked and you just need a pick me up from someone in the business. K9 Businesses also offers forums, question and answer support and can help you both in the creation of your business and throughout the lifetime of your business.

I thought I would share some rules for success from an extremely established business owner, Steve Jobs of the Apple corporation. He gave his employees a set of rules for success, I feel that these also resonate with the owner of a small business and could help you as you progress through the creation of your company and through your career.

Rules for Success

- ⇒ Let go of the old, make the most of the future
- ⇒ Always tell the truth
- ⇒ Maintain the highest level of integrity, when in doubt, ask
- ⇒ Learn to be a good businessperson, not just a good salesperson
- ⇒ Everyone sweeps the floor
- ⇒ Be professional in your style, speech and follow-up
- ⇒ Listen to the customer
- ⇒ Create win/win relationships
- ⇒ Look out for each other, sharing of information is a good thing
- ⇒ Don't take yourself too seriously
- ⇒ Have fun, otherwise it's not worth it

Taken from Business Insider article by Kif Leswing, (2017).

Chapter 14

Why do I need- Insurance?

Why do I need- Insurance?

Why do I need insurance for a dog walking company? All professional businesses have some type of Insurance, the same goes for a dog walking company. It is important to remember that working with dogs, like any animal, involves risk and can be dangerous. Especially when working with people's beloved dogs you are in a trusted position with tons of emotion and financial responsibility. Dog walking business insurance covers lots of different facets centring around dog walking public liability and often optional accident and injury cover as these are the most common and expensive things that could happen to you as a dog walker. Examples could include a dog causing an accident or injury to somebody, damage to someone else's property, a dog is injured or lost, or a dog is accidently injured when it was not your fault. It is also valuable to take out loss of key cover, should you lose a client's key, most insurers will cover the cost of replacing their locks. As you progress in your business there are also additional optional extras such as equipment cover, and employer's liability cover should you take someone on to help you.

It is essential that you understand the terms discussed within insurance quotes and read the small print carefully. There are many different pet business insurers with different prices. Like you do with car insurance/ home insurance, ring round different providers for quotes or look online. If you do not understand a term, ask – you need to know what it is that you are buying.

What is Public liability insurance? Essentially, public liability is there if a member of the public claimed compensation for injury or damage caused by your business (including that caused by a dog in your care). Your public liability insurance can protect you and help you to battle legal cases and cover fees. Compensation in these types of claims can often run into millions of pounds, it is therefore extremely important that when you take out a policy it is the best cover you can get. Most insurers offer cover for between £1 million and £10 million pounds.

Specific insurance for your pet business. There are many types of pet businesses, therefore it is important to ensure that you get business that covers dog walkers. Some insurers can cover for injury to pets as part of your public liability insurance, this means that if a pet was injured or became ill whilst in your care, your policy would protect you from a customer claim. It is something to look out for whilst choosing your pet business insurer.

Business equipment cover is usually for pet businesses like groomers. However, some policies cover the equipment such as leads, harnesses, seatbelts etc of dog walkers. Check your policy wording or simply ask when getting quotes. This addition would cover you for immediate losses such as if there was a theft or equipment was lost or stolen. The equipment generally used for day-to-day dog walking is usually relatively cheap so you must decide for yourself whether this addition is worth the extra money.

Personal accident and Injury are a huge part of pet business cover. If you are working with animals on a day to day basis, you will at some point during your career end up getting injured or having an accident. Costs that are incurred by accidents can quickly sore, especially if the accident or injury results in loss of earnings, limbs or death. The money paid out can cover your loss of earnings, enable you to seek private medical care and help with costs of treatment.

Think carefully about insurers and ask other professionals who they are covered by. Do your research, read small print carefully, get quotes and compare.

Chapter 15

Accountants and HMRC

Accountants and HMRC

If you are self-employed, you are legally obliged to register with the HMRC [UK only] (Her Majesty's Revenue and Customs so that they can calculate your earnings and collect the appropriate amount of tax owed to the state.

The HMRC provide a list of indicators that define what being self-employed is, they are as follows.

- Run your own Business
- Have more than 1 customer simultaneously
- You decide how and when you work
- You have the option to hire others
- You provide most of the equipment needed for your work
- You take responsibility for completing unfinished work or unsatisfactory work in your own time
- You charge a fixed price for your work, agreed with a client or customer
- You sell goods or a service for profit (this excludes selling unwanted items on an ad-hoc basis)

Registering self-employed requires you to register for a Government Gateway account. This grants you access to a range of online services, especially the part that is the HMRC's Self-Assessment Portal, visit https://www.gov.uk/log-in-register-hmrc-online-services to register.

Once you have registered, your details are sent by post, you then have 90 days to activate you login for the fist time. After you have done this, you are required to complete a range of details about you and your business, including contact details and the type of work that you do. Here you will also need to add the name of your business. Most people just register under their own name, but you can register your business name as a trading name. If you are doing this, you need to make sure that there are no other existing businesses using the same name to avoid confusion.

According to the HMRC, you should register as soon as possible, however there is a legal deadline to register by the 5th October of the second business trading year. You need to carefully consider leaving your registration this long though as if anything goes wrong and you struggle to register you could find yourself with a very hefty tax bill.

There is a difference between a sole-trader and self-employed. If you work by yourself, on your own you are probably a sole-trader and should register as so; there are more options than just sole trader. If you are in a business partnership, you would need to register as self-employed and not a sole trader. Instead you register as a partner. You could register as a limited company too, but things get a little more complicated as you then become both an owner of a company and an employee. For more clarification on the differences see the HMRC government website.

Once you are registered as self-employed there are certain legal obligations you must complete. The most crucial of which is keeping adequate records particularly of sales and outgoings connected to your business. This should then be filed in a Self-Assessment Tax Return which needs to be completed by 31st January every year. Payments for tax are paid in two intervals throughout the year, once on the 31st January and again on the 31st July. In addition to the tax payment, you will also have to pay a National Insurance contribution (class 2 and class 4).

This is all if you are going to do the self-assessment tax return yourself, there is a much simpler option, but it does come with a cost. You could employ an accountant. You need to look carefully for an accountant, compare prices and how they can help you. There are many accountants out there who specialise in small business tax. It is these types of accountant who will work best for dog walking companies as usually their costs are lower and more flexible than corporate giants. They also consider the minimal expenses incurred to smaller business and will process these along with your tax return. Look for locally recommended accountants or ask other dog walkers which accountant they use, personal recommendation, like with the development of your business, mean for a much more reliable services as it has been tried and tested by others.

When completing your self-assessment or filing your accounts with your accountant. You will need copies of items listed below.

Accountants and HMRC Checklist

- Invoices for the year
- Bank Statements
- Expenses Receipts (no matter how small)
- Mileage Log

Further Reading

- Animal Welfare Act 2006
- Antisocial Behaviour, Crime and Policing Act 2014
- Canine Enrichment & Corona Virus 2020
- Code of Practice for the welfare of Dogs 2017
- The Control of Dogs Order 1992
- Countryside & Right of Way Act 2000
- Dangerous Dog Act 1991
- Data Protection Act 2018
- The Dangerous Dogs (Amendment) Act 1997
- Dogs (Fouling of Land) Act 1996
- Dog Fouling & Clean Neighbourhoods and Environment Act 2005
- Dogs Protection of Livestock Act 1953
- Environmental Protection Act 1990
- Health and Safety (First Aid) Regulations 1981
- Health and Safety at Work Act 1974
- Management of Health and Safety at Work Regulations 1999
- The Microchipping of Dogs (England) Regulations 2015

Further Reading Continued

- Model Licence Conditions and Guidance for Dog Boarding Establishments 2016
- Personal Protective Equipment at Work Regulations 1992
- Regulation on The Protection of Animals During Transport 1/2005
- Welfare of Animals (Transport) (England) Order 2006
- Workplace (Health, Safety and Welfare) Regulations 1992
- www.creativecommons.org

Printed in Great Britain
by Amazon

16357078R00050